E220196943

CU01401525

HOW TO BE AN EARTHLING

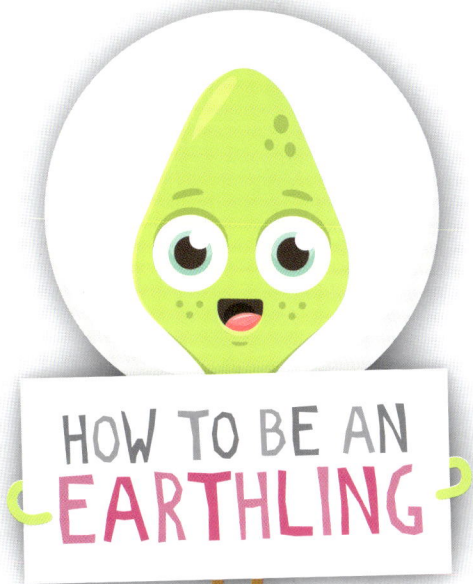

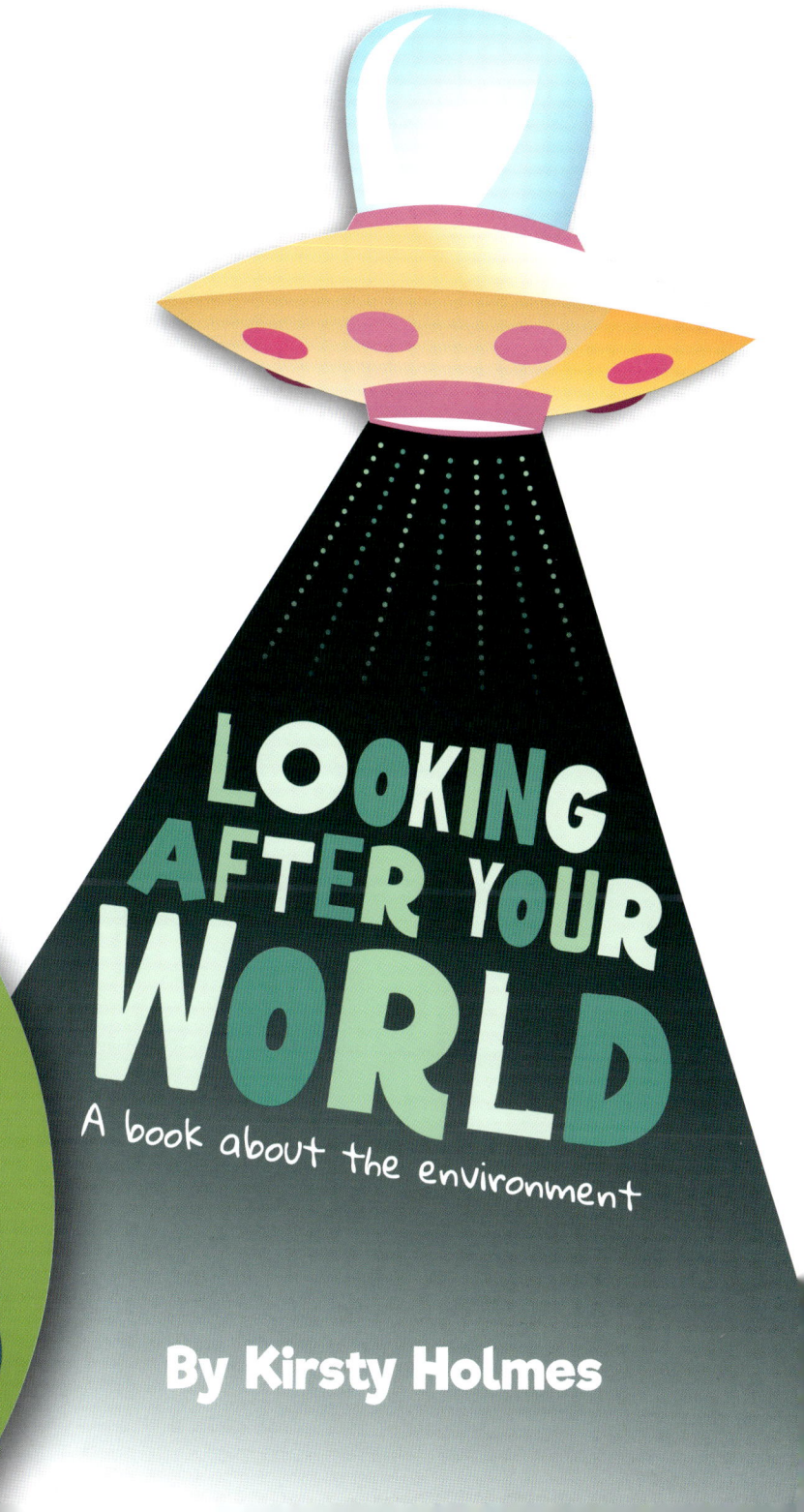

LOOKING AFTER YOUR WORLD

A book about the environment

By Kirsty Holmes

BookLife
PUBLISHING

©2020
BookLife Publishing Ltd.
King's Lynn
Norfolk, PE30 4LS

ISBN: 978-1-78637-982-5

Written by:
Kirsty Holmes

Edited by:
Madeline Tyler

Designed by:
Dan Scase

PHOTO CREDITS

All images are courtesy of Shutterstock.com, unless otherwise specified. With thanks to Getty Images, Thinkstock Photo and iStockphoto.
Front Cover – Tomacco, delcarmat, Roi and Roi, Subbotina Anna, Dmytro Zinkevych, sarayut_sy, PremiumArt, Monphoto. 4&5 – BEST-BACKGROUNDS, YUCALORA. 6&7 – Anton Petrus, jeremykingnz, Neale Cousland, Luciano Cosmo, Harvepino. 8&9 – Vector8DIY, Peangdao, pasindufx, IgorZh, Ondrej Prosicky, Pavel Svoboda Photography, karamysh, Popova Tetiana. 10&11 – LilKar, Monkey Business Images. 12&13 – Sergiy Palamarchuk, EpicStockMedia, Fedorov Oleksiy, Marten_House, Hung Chung Chih, NadyGinzburg, Neil Mitchell. 14&15 – Rich Carey, dimitris_k, stockphoto-graf, Rich Carey. 16&17 – AustralianCamera, ALEX_UGALEK, Creative Travel Projects, Ozerov Alexander, Rich Carey. 18&19 – YUCALORA, Ruslana Iurchenko, narikan. 20&21 – majeczka, Smileus, Constantine Androsoff, Rawpixel.com. 22 – Mladen Zivkovic, My Life Graphic. Alien Bo – delcarmat. Alien Zop – Roi and Roi. Background – PremiumArt. Vectors throughout – kearia. Speech bubbles – Surrphoto.

CONTENTS

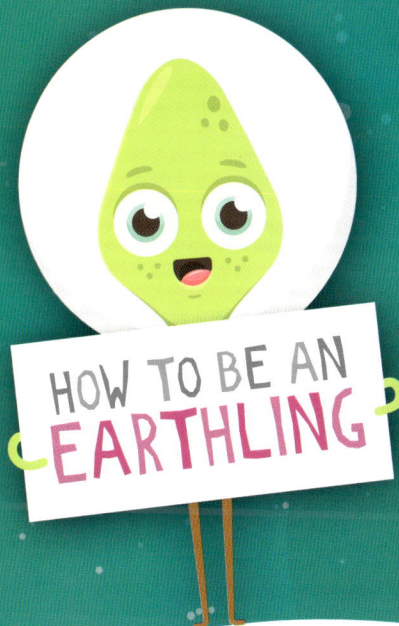

HOW TO BE AN EARTHLING

Words that look like this can be found in the glossary on page 24.

SOMEWHERE IN THE SOLAR SYSTEM...

Look up into the night sky. Can you see it? One star is shining brighter than all the others. Is it a star? It could be a <u>satellite</u>. Or it could be... an alien spaceship!

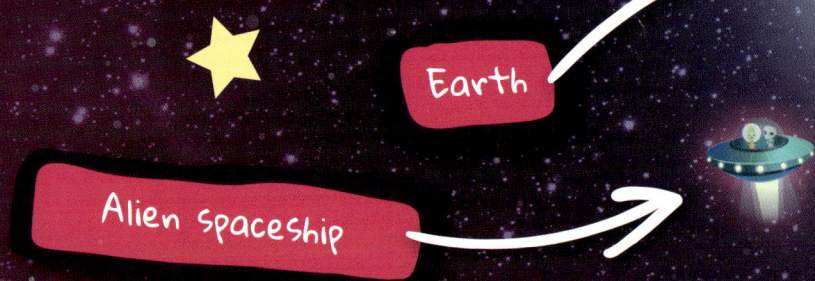

Earth

Alien spaceship

Two plucky aliens from the Omega Quadrant are on a mission to the planet Earth. Bo and Zop must learn all about the Earthlings who live there and see if they are safe to visit.

I'm Bo. Can we land? I feel sick.

I'm Zop! Look at all these trees!

Today, Bo and Zop are looking for a good place on Earth to land. They want to build a home for all their friends from Omegatron.

Too hot...

Too cold...

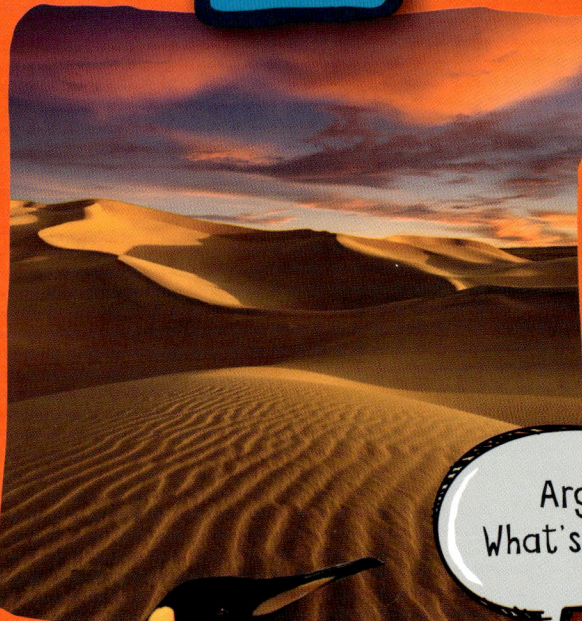

Argh! What's that?

I think it's called a penguin.

6

The Amazon rainforest

It's perfect! All we need to do is get rid of all those big green things.

Do you mean the trees? That would be bad for the environment, Bo!

Bo thinks he has found a good spot. It has the right climate and lots of space. There is only one problem...

HOME SWEET HOME

Wherever the Earthlings live, they are surrounded by the environment. The environment is made up of lots of things, such as:

What is the environment, anyway?

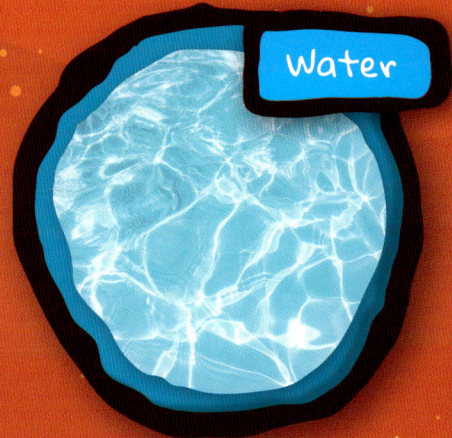
Water

Weather

Air

Plants and trees

Animals

Earthlings live all over planet Earth. All their homes look different. Some are cold and snowy. Some are green and bright. Others are dry and nothing much can grow there.

Greenland

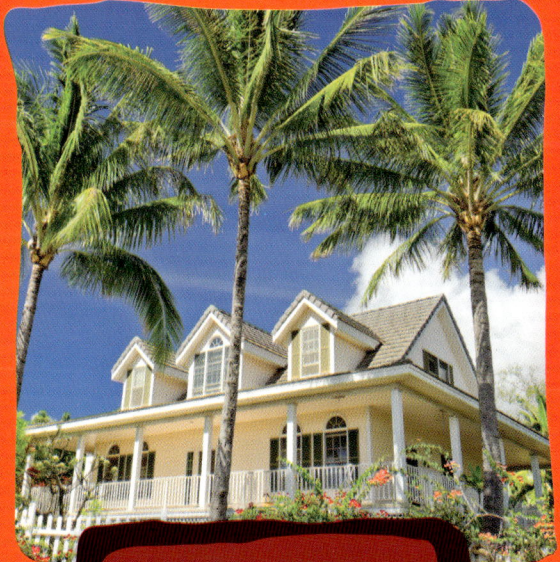

Hawaii, US

9

To live and be happy, Earthlings need air to breathe, food to eat, water to drink, shelter to protect them from the weather, and warmth from heat sources such as the Sun and fires.

Everything that humans need can be found in the environment.

There are over 7 billion Earthlings on planet Earth. Many of them live separately from the natural environment. They live in houses and flats, get water from the tap, and heat their homes without fires.

There are some problems with living like this, though.

EARTH IN TROUBLE

Food is grown on farms

Fossil fuels are taken from the ground

Earthlings living in houses might not be foraging for food in the forests or lighting fires, but they still get the things they need from the environment.

Materials for building are dug up

Trees are cut down to make space

Ok, so what's the problem?

Well, the way this is done can be very bad for the environment.

Factories, cars and power stations can all cause <u>pollution</u>. The air becomes dirty and is not good for Earthlings to breathe.

13

Plastic waste

All these Earthlings make a lot of rubbish. A lot of this rubbish ends up in the oceans and rivers. The water quickly becomes polluted, dirty and not safe for Earthlings to use.

Oil spills

Sewage

Pollution in the water is very bad for the animals and plants that live there. If the water is polluted, the Earthlings can't drink it, and they can't catch and eat the fish either.

Don't Earthlings need water to live?

Yes, they do. And lots of them eat fish too.

Trees are very important to life on planet Earth. They clean the air, help save water and keep the soil in place.

When large areas of forest are cut down to make space for other things, it is called deforestation. Animals lose their homes, and the soil is blown or washed away.

Oh look! Can we put the base camp there? They've cut all the trees down!

That's a bad thing, Bo. That is a lot of damage to the environment.

ZOP TO THE RESCUE

By the time we set up base camp, there will be nothing left of this planet. We might as well go home.

Well, not yet, Bo. There is some hope...

Many Earthlings know that they need to protect the environment. They have been learning to do things in new ways that will not hurt the environment.

Earth is the only home they have, so all Earthlings need to take care of it. Bo and Zop will need to look for ways to build a home that aren't bad for the environment.

All Earthlings living together...

... in <u>harmony</u> with the environment!

MAKING CHOICES

Water power uses <u>dams</u>

Solar power uses the Sun's energy

Luckily, those clever Earthlings have come up with some brilliant ways of looking after the planet.

Wind power uses wind

There are now lots of ways to make power that don't damage the environment. This is called renewable energy.

Earthlings should use as little plastic as possible. We should recycle any plastic we do use. This means it is turned into a new material that can be used again.

That's a great idea!

AN ECO HOME

Can you plan an environmentally friendly home for Bo, Zop and their friends? Where could you build it? What materials could you use? How could you make power?

Bo understands now. He has drawn a plan of an environmentally friendly base for himself and Zop.

That looks like a great place to live.

We have to look after the environment, Zop!

GLOSSARY

CLIMATE	the common weather in a certain place
DAMS	barriers that hold back the water in a river or stream
EARTHLINGS	human beings
FORAGING	looking for food
FOSSIL FUELS	fuels, such as coal, oil and gas, which formed millions of years ago from the remains of animals and plants
HARMONY	getting along
PLUCKY	brave and adventurous
POLLUTION	when harmful or poisonous things get into the environment
SATELLITE	a machine in space that travels around planets, taking photographs and collecting and sending information to Earth
SEWAGE	waste water from homes and factories that often includes human waste

INDEX